THE BEEHOUSE BOOK

Paul Mann

Northern Bee Books

The Beehouse Book

ISBN 978-1-904846-67-3

Published by Northern Bee Books
Scout Bottom Farm,
Mytholmroyd,
Hebden Bridge
West Yorkshire HX7 5JS

Design and Artwork
D&P Design and Print
Set in Adobe Jenson Pro

Printed and bound in Great Britain by
Lightning Source UK

THE BEEHOUSE BOOK

Paul Mann

I should like to dedicate this book to my wife Josie,
and all my family for their patience over the years.
Also to all the beekeepers I have met and
for their company and friendship

Northern Bee Books

*"Why is there always too much
week/month left at the end of the money"*

THE BEEHOUSE BOOK.

INTRODUCTION.

Beekeepers are very anthropomorphic when it comes to their bees. They imagine the bees in the hive down the garden "think as they do", during frosty weather they will say to themselves "The bees must feel very cold, I will go and put some extra insulation to keep them warmer". This has manifested itself by various ways, one is to keep the bees within some sort of building. There are examples of this over the years, bee boles, an open fronted shed or within a stone or brick building. In "Bee Boles and beehouses", see below there are several types shown from previous years. The beehouse at Attingham Park was built in the early 1800's before frame hives came into use. There has been an excellent restoration carried out and the last time I visited there were skeps with bees in residence. It is well worth a visit if you are in the area, it is a few miles East of Shrewsbury on the old A5.

Pictures of beehouse at Attingham Park, showing detail. *Photographs by the author*

While on the subject of skeps, I re-call a meeting, many years ago, where the speaker was very late. The chairman filled in with the following story, I am sure it was passed down. Beekeepers during the days before frame hives would keep their skeps on a long board, 10 to 15 in a row. When the keeper decided to take the honey crop they would go along the row and "heft", check the weight, of each skep. Heavy ones would be pulled back, they contained a good crop. Very light ones would also be pulled back, they were unlikely to last the winter. Medium ones would be pushed forwards; they would make it through the coming winter and provide next years colonies and hopefully swarms. This was how beekeepers of the day increased their number of colonies. A balance had to be struck to have enough colonies for the following year. The skeps were left until evening when a pit would be dug; the diameter of the skeps and some 18 inches [450mm] deep, combustible material was put in the hole and sulphur sprinkled on top. The fire was lit, the skeps were now carried from the bench to the pit and held over the fire until all buzzing ceased, the bees were dead. All the skeps at the back of the bench followed.

The combs were now cut out and sorted into those containing honey and those with brood, the later to be melted down. The kitchen table was turned upside down and a clean sheet tied to the tops of the four legs A large bowl was placed under the sheet. The pieces of comb were now crushed and placed in the sheet; the whole was drawn up to the fire to heat the honey so that it would drain through more quickly. In time the honey crop was in the bowl and the empty wax combs would be melted down. I thought this was a marvellous description of a time long ago in the world of beekeeping, frame hives have changed all that.

Killing the bees was frowned on, as it would be to-day, and someone thought of the idea of "driving" the bees out of condemned skeps. The occupied skep was turned up side down and stood in a bucket, an empty skep was fastened at the rear with a skewer and two large staples were pushed in each side so that a gap about 45 degrees was made. The beekeeper now sat in front of the skep and drummed the sides steadily with both hands; this caused the bees to walk up into the top skep. The honey could now be harvested without the bees being killed and the bees could be added to weak colonies.

"driving" bees

Bees are cold blooded creatures; they take up the temperature around them. If this gets too low they will cluster and those in the centre will generate heat which will permeate out to the surface of the cluster. So long as they have an adequate supply of food they will survive. Bees are kept in Canada and Russia where much colder temperature are experienced than Britain. In spite of this beekeepers over the years have built protection for their hives and bees.

There are two inherent problems, the bees flying within the beehouse cannot find their way out satisfactorily and the light level inside is too low, this means that the beekeeper cannot inspect the contents of the brood combs. In Beecraft May 2003 I wrote an article about my beehouses, much of it is included in this offering. The article created much interest with many sets of plans being sent out. I have wondered how many beehouses were in fact built.

BEE SHED; INTERNAL, BOX POSITION.

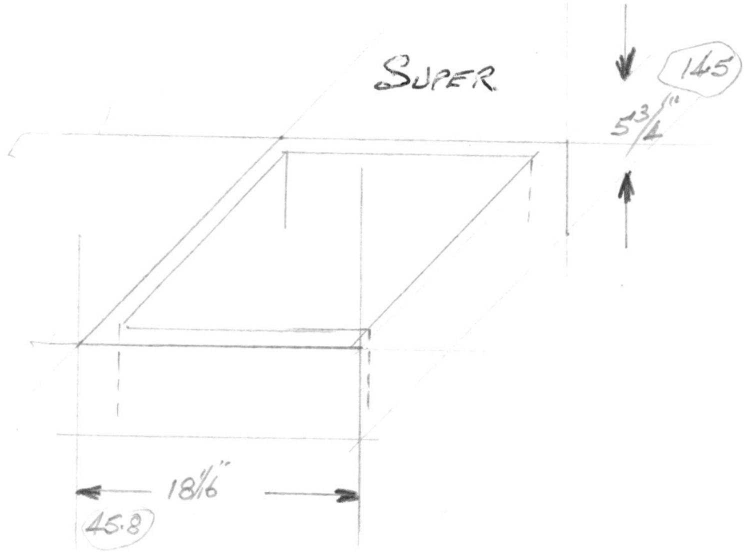

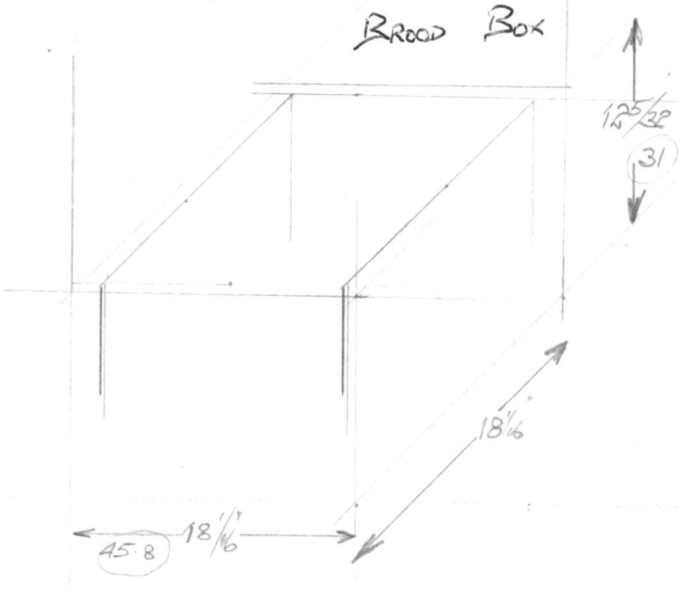

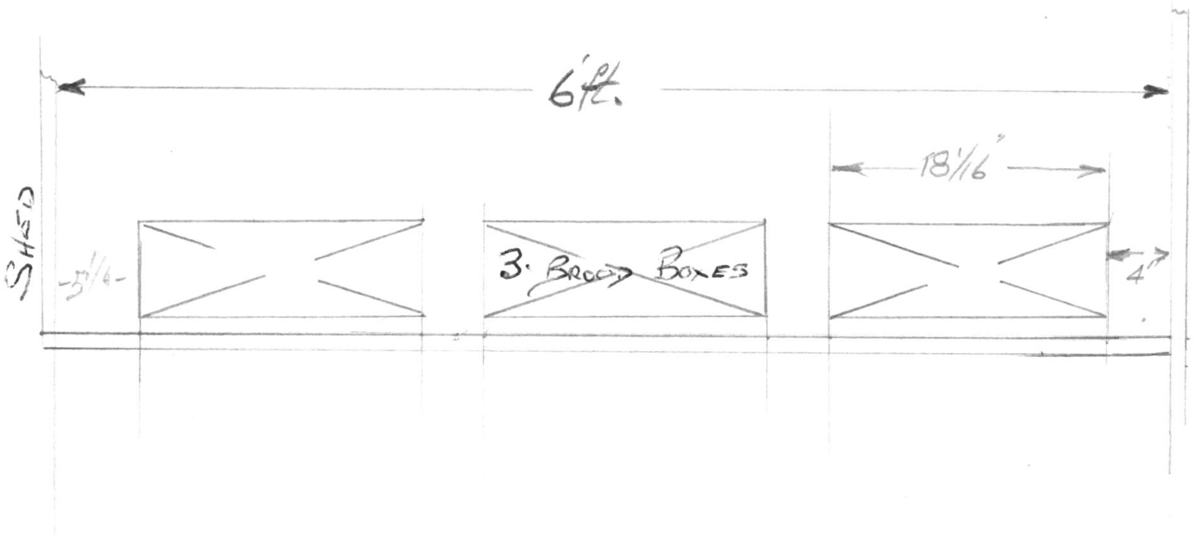

SUPER

145

$5\frac{3}{4}''$

$18\frac{1}{6}''$

45.8

BROOD BOX

$12\frac{25}{32}$

31

$18\frac{1}{6}$

$18\frac{1}{6}''$

45.8

6 ft.

$18\frac{1}{6}''$

SHED

$5\frac{3}{4}-$

3. BROOD BOXES

4"

RULE :- "D"

Bee Shed; Wall Interanl.

Bee Shed; Wall Interanl.

6ft

18⅛"   6"

3'-7"

Super.   5¾"

12⁵⁄₁₆

Brood Box.

Floor.
Bench.   1⅗₁₆

24"

Storage   13"

Floor.

6ft. inside mersurement.

Shed Wall.

My own beekeeping started in 1942 with my father being the instigator with me following on. I was always looking in the Birmingham Central Library for bee books and they had a very good collection. Among these I found "Beekeeping New and Old", by Herrod Hempsall. This book was very large and heavy, it contained many pictures. Dad was always a keen exhibitor at any shows which took his fancy. In 1944 he had an observation hive made, 6 British standard brood frames and 2 shallows above. It was quite large and heavy to get up and down stairs. It was also difficult to get into a car. We lived near the middle of Birmingham in a built up area. The only way we could have bees at home was for them to be upstairs so that they flew out over the small back garden. It was decided that the observation hive should be in my bedroom at the rear of the house. A table was set up under a sash window which was about 6 feet tall and 3 ft wide. A tunnel with a glass top connected the hive to the window under the sash. It provided hours of interest watching the bees coming and going. The only problems occurred when the hive was opened, most of the bees went out through the open window but a few would end up on the floor. I found some of these at a later time. Later I had bees in a shed, to try my hand at queen rearing, with the usual problems, the difficulty of bees getting outside again and seeing the contents of a brood comb. With side windows it is almost impossible to have sufficient light to see into a brood comb. It becomes necessary to take the frame outside to see the contents.

Later I felt there had to be a better way. There had to be an opening above to let in sufficient light for the beekeeper to work and at the same time enable the flying bees to get out. I had seen the inside of a number of touring caravans with lantern roofs; these provided good lighting, often in the kitchen area. This seemed to be the way to go. We had been using a 16foot touring caravan and I think this influenced me to suggest 32 colonies in one beehouse At the same time I thought it could be a good idea if the beehouses could be moved from site to site. I had also seen poultry houses on skids which could be pulled around a field by a tractor. These gave me an idea for a portable beehouse. The picture shows how my first ideas where put on paper on Weymouth beach while on holiday. It may seem strange to be doing this while on holiday but I have found that it is a good time for thought, away from the activities of normal life. The body of the beehouse would be built on two skids so it could be moved and loaded onto a trailer. Once erected and bolted together the beehouse is very rigid and can be moved about without distorting to any extent. As far as I know no commercial beekeeper has ever used this idea. The design has solid sides [no windows] with entrances through the sides for access for the bees. The lantern roof is to provide an escape for bees leaving open hives and ventilation and a very good light source. I was living in Lancashire at the time and selling equipment for Thorne's. I built the first one and put it on display so that customers for equipment had to walk past. Over the next 10 years I sold about 12 of these beehouses and the customers seemed quite pleased.

"A certificate is like a box of tools. Now let us see if you use them."

PREVIOUS PUBLICATIONS

"THE HOUSE APIARY" BY JOHN SPILLER was published around 1947. It retailed for 12/6 [62 new pence] and contained 56 pages. New copies are still available I gather. There are five photographs of the outsides of his beehouses and two of their interiors. There are extra pictures and sketches of the internal arrangements. All the beehouses have solid roofs and side windows, most are converted chicken houses. Normal outdoor hives were used inside. I was very impressed by the lifting arrangements for supers or other heavy boxes. An "H" section bar is above the hives with a slider to move along the bar. The lifting unit is a rope with compound pulleys; I have seen these in use on sailing boats to haul the sails tight. I shall bear this in mind for the future. Interesting as the book is, I cannot see anyone now using such a beehouse.

Spiller Beehouse - Page 12

John Spiller in 1910 - Page 40

"BEE BOLES AND BEE HOUSES" by A.M.Foster is No 204 in the Shire Album Series and published by Shire Publications Ltd. Still available at £4.99. The first 19 pages cover Bee Boles, then 3 pages of bee shelters and 3 pages of beehouses. It has 32 pages with many old pictures.

The picture on page 3 shows a beekeeper extracting honey outside a beehouse showing 10 entrances. The extractor would appear to be 1930's and the frame propped up against the extractor looks like a 16 in by 10 in, a British Commercial as we now know them. The picture is from the Alfred Watkins collection which is held at Hereford City Library. There are quite a few beekeeping pictures from the early 1900, they can be copied for the price of the print.

"AN INTRODUCTION TO BEEHOUSES". This booklet written and published by DAVID BATES is undated but as it is still on sale so it must be more recent. It has 39 pages and is available from Northern Bee Books at £5.00. Again it shows pictures of beehouses converted from a garden sheds, solid roof and side windows. Interestingly at the end of the book is a sketch of a beehouse showing an "Opening roof light and bee escape", below is says "We all have dreams". I think I have found the way to fulfil these dreams.

David Bates has clearly seen and been converted to the continental type of bee hive where they are opened from the rear. I feel that we already have far too many types of hive in Britain without adding more. It is still very confusing for beginners; they have to choose a type of hive without any experience or knowledge on which to base the choice. When they ask for advice they will receive so much conflicting information that they are probably even more confused. We need a web site. www.whichhive.com . If we only had one type it would be so much easier. In my view!!

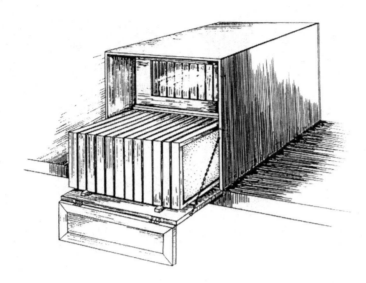

This diagram (above), taken from page 15 of "An introduction to Bee-Houses" shows the general arrangement. The rear door drops down or is removed in some cases. The frames are then worked on as required. I have never seen this in action but Propolis and burr comb must be a problem, particularly if the hive has not been looked at for a while".

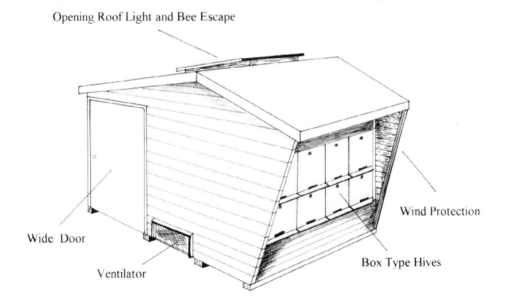

Opening Roof Light and Bee Escape

Wind Protection

Wide Door

Ventilator

Box Type Hives

"DRAWINGS FOR A beehouse" by John Phipps. It is a solid pent roof shed with side windows so the same old problems will be present. To my mind a clear panel in the roof is essential for a beehouse to be acceptable to the beekeeper.

The continental beehouse shown on page 8 and 9 is of this type, I can count 33 openings so we must assume that at times 33 colonies are housed in the structure. The continental hives have two compartments, the lower one is used as a brood chamber and above this is a queen excluder to restrict the queen's movement. On top is a similar compartment used as a honey area. The hives can be stacked one above the other and side by side, this makes full use of the available space. The rear of the hive is closed by a door, which is opened when the beekeeper is working on the colony. The frames are the cold way so one is faced with the ends of the frames, these have to be removed to examine the brood area and to replace or exchange the combs. The honey crop is taken from the box above frame by frame as they are capped. I presume the extractor is in use most of the time during the honey flow.

Large continental beehouse

"You cannot buy happiness but it is nice to be miserable in comfort"

GENERAL ARRANGEMENT OF
MY TYPE OF BEEHOUSE.

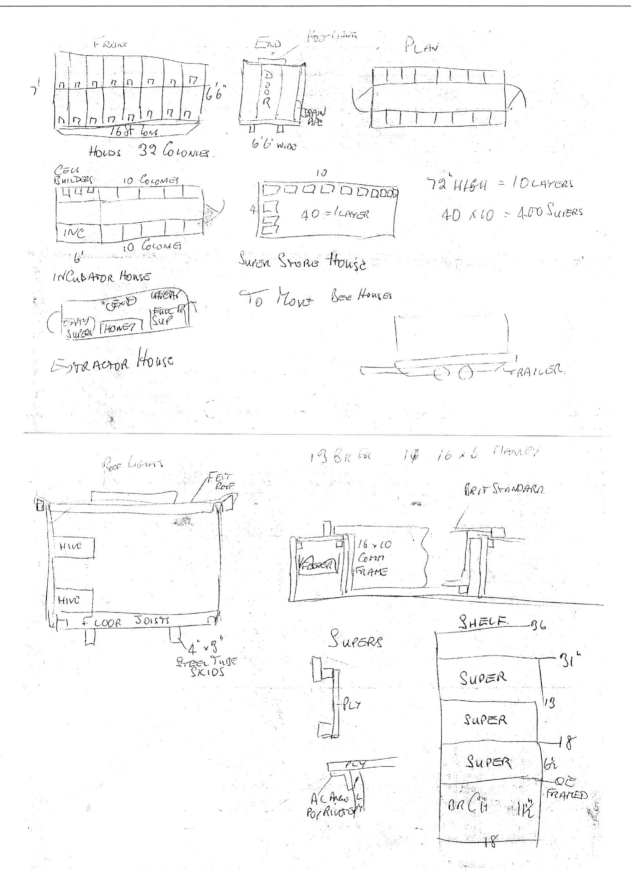

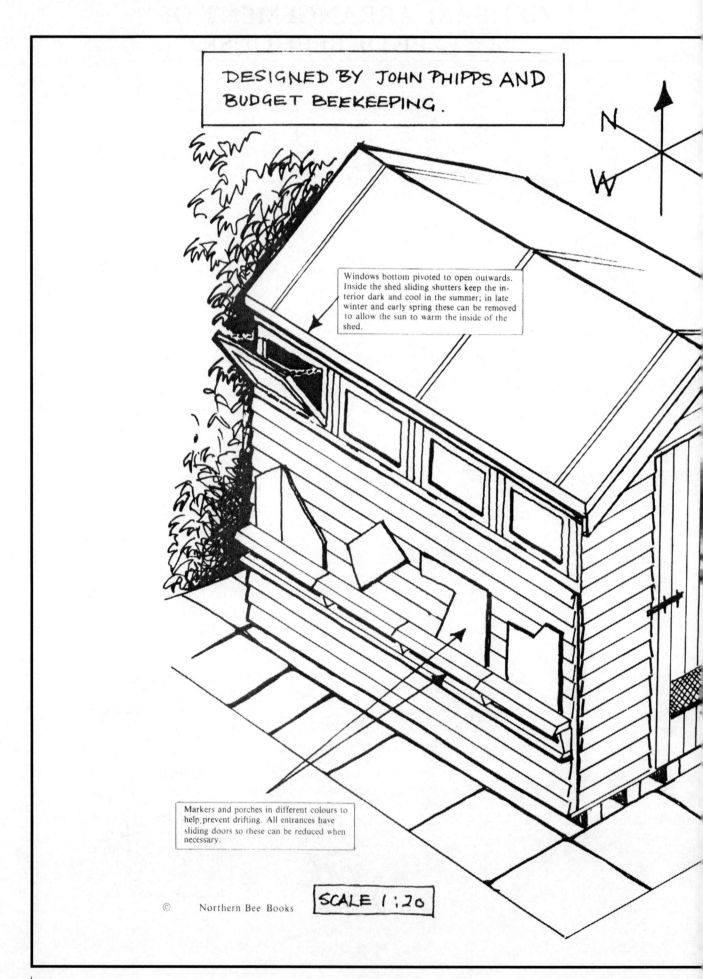

DESIGNED BY JOHN PHIPPS AND BUDGET BEEKEEPING.

Windows bottom pivoted to open outwards. Inside the shed sliding shutters keep the interior dark and cool in the summer; in late winter and early spring these can be removed to allow the sun to warm the inside of the shed.

Markers and porches in different colours to help prevent drifting. All entrances have sliding doors so these can be reduced when necessary.

© Northern Bee Books

SCALE 1:20

CONTINENTAL BEEHOUSE
by John Phipps

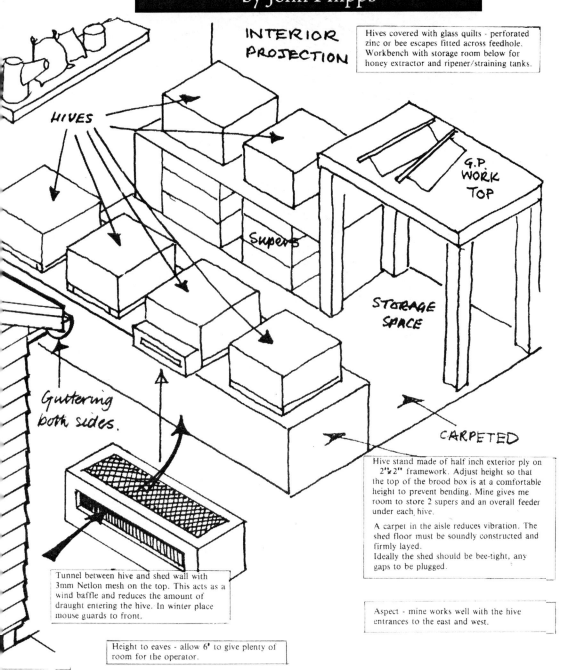

INTERIOR PROJECTION

Hives covered with glass quilts - perforated zinc or bee escapes fitted across feedhole. Workbench with storage room below for honey extractor and ripener/straining tanks.

HIVES

G.P. WORK TOP

Supers

STORAGE SPACE

Guttering both sides.

CARPETED

Hive stand made of half inch exterior ply on 2"x 2" framework. Adjust height so that the top of the brood box is at a comfortable height to prevent bending. Mine gives me room to store 2 supers and an overall feeder under each hive.

A carpet in the aisle reduces vibration. The shed floor must be soundly constructed and firmly layed.
Ideally the shed should be bee-tight, any gaps to be plugged.

Tunnel between hive and shed wall with 3mm Netlon mesh on the top. This acts as a wind baffle and reduces the amount of draught entering the hive. In winter place mouse guards to front.

Aspect - mine works well with the hive entrances to the east and west.

Height to eaves - allow 6' to give plenty of room for the operator.

of ventilator - one is located pex of the l.

An at a Glance Guide to: Keeping Bees in a Bee House

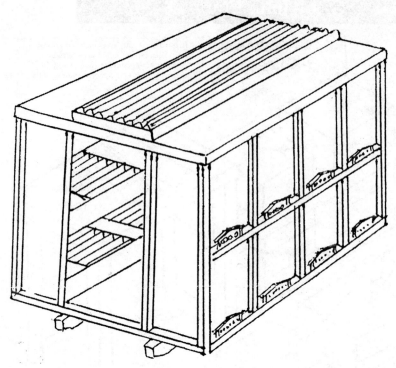

General view showing the skids, entrances, internal hives and plastic roof

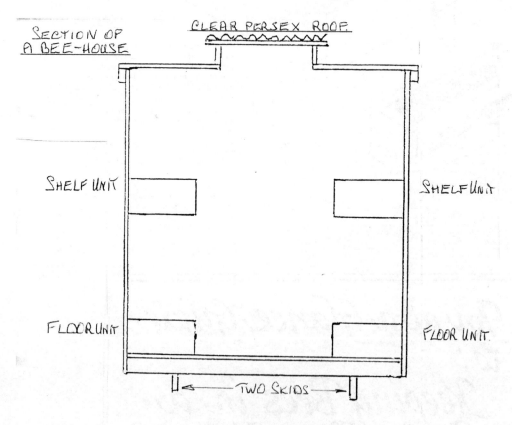

Section showing shelf units

Earlier I have shown how my design came about. I considered that 16ft length too great so 8 feet became the maximum. I have a high regard for plywood so that the main components are designed around an 8fet by 4 feet sheet.[Now 2400mm by 1200mm]. I started at the roof which was to be a sheet cut down the centre; this would have a 2 foot [600mm] gap to provide the light source. This set the dimensions of the sides and floor. Now the height, I took 6 feet [1800mm] as this would allow two layers of hive with room for three supers on each colony. Most of the beehouses that I made were to these dimensions. The one shown [below] is 8 feet [2400mm] high, this was for a customer who wished to use double brood boxes. It does make full use of a ply sheet but steps or a box may be needed to reach the top.

This picture shows the inside of an 8 ft high beehouse with the two layers of hives clearly visible. As this beekeeper wished to use double brood boxes and several supers the top layers were screwed to the sides and I supplied a support to go half way along. As I heard no more I assume this arrangement was successful

The most popular was the 8' by 6'; the 8 feet length would accommodate 4 colonies on two levels on each side. 16 colonies in 48 square feet is very economical. The frames were the warm way to make removal easier. The 4 colonies were housed in a single unit of 4 brood chambers between two side members again of plywood.

Standard supers can be used or lighter construction similar to those used in W.B.C. hives. The top needs to be closed by a crown board. If left open the bees will use this as an entrance and fly through the roof.

These arrangements fulfilled the two main problems. Any bees loose in the beehouse could escape quickly through the gaps around the roof and the beekeeper has excellent light to work and see the contents of the frames. The light was so good that I found that I could even do my grafting inside the beehouse, quite warm and no wind.

At the time I had a saw bench, wood working tools and adequate space. Please note I am not a carpenter. I think every potential beekeeper should do a wood working course while still at school. I wish I had but the combination of subjects did not allow this. My design gives a flat smooth inside face to each wall. The structural framework is on the outside, this needs to be regularly treated with preservative to give a long life.

USING TRADITIONAL HIVES INSIDE
A BEEHOUSE.

Any of the single wall hives can be pushed against the wall. The internal boxes of W.B.C hives could be used in the same way, it would be essential for these to be bee tight where boxes meet. Using traditional hives for a second layer would require a substantial shelf to support them.

I found that "built-in" hives were very satisfactory. Originally these were built into a non sectional prototype. The sectional production beehouses had units of 4 brood boxes [or as appropriate for the smaller beehouses]. The picture shows a set of 4 brood boxes ready to be built in. If you will picture two sides fastened to this unit you will have a substantial coffin type assembly which will sit on the beehouse floor.

I found that two layers of hives worked really well. The upper layer sits on supports at each end. For added strength screws or thin bolts can be used to secure the sides of the beehouse to the hive unit. This helps to make the sides more rigid.

GENERAL ARRANGEMENT

The diagrams and pictures show the general arrangement. The floor supports the rest of the building and the hives within. A very good crop of honey, every beekeepers dream would make the hives and contents over 200 LBS [180Kg] each. I have used ply and chipboard for the floor. Ply is more expensive but more stable. Chipboard attracts moisture during the winter period and this causes swelling of the board. I prefer to use bolts, screws or ring nails to hold timber together. Ring nails may be new to some of you, they are like a screw without a thread, and they are used extensively on pallets. Once driven home they are almost impossible to remove. You have been warned. My father used to tell me "measure it twice and cut it once", very sound advice. The same applies to ring nails, only drive them once.

The plans show a very substantial floor, the construction is heavy when completed. If you are absolutely sure that the beehouse will never ever need to be moved then it could be lighter. If you take this route then think of the affect of any dimension changes. The most important dimensions are the length and breadth of the floor, the sides need to "FIT" around the floor and the roof needs to "FIT" around the sides.

As the floor is 6ft wide you will need to join up two pieces of ply. Tongue and groove ply is available for floors, but more expensive. Square edged ply should have a support to join the sheets together. Treat the under parts with a preservative as it may be in contact with damp soil.

To build the panels you will need a flat clean area in which to work. It would be very cramped in a single garage but a double garage would be ideal. A patio or drive could be used but the weather may take a hand at times.

The sides are very similar, do please make sure you make them "handed". When placed together the slope of the roof should match. It is very, very annoying if you get it wrong!!!".

A completed beehouse on site

For beekeepers who find it difficult to get their bees "right" each year.

"Write down the year of your death, underneath put the current year. Take bottom from top. The answer is the number of years you have to get it right."

"If you think you can you will.
If you think you can't you won't.
The wo[man] who wins is the
wo[man] who thinks s[he] can".

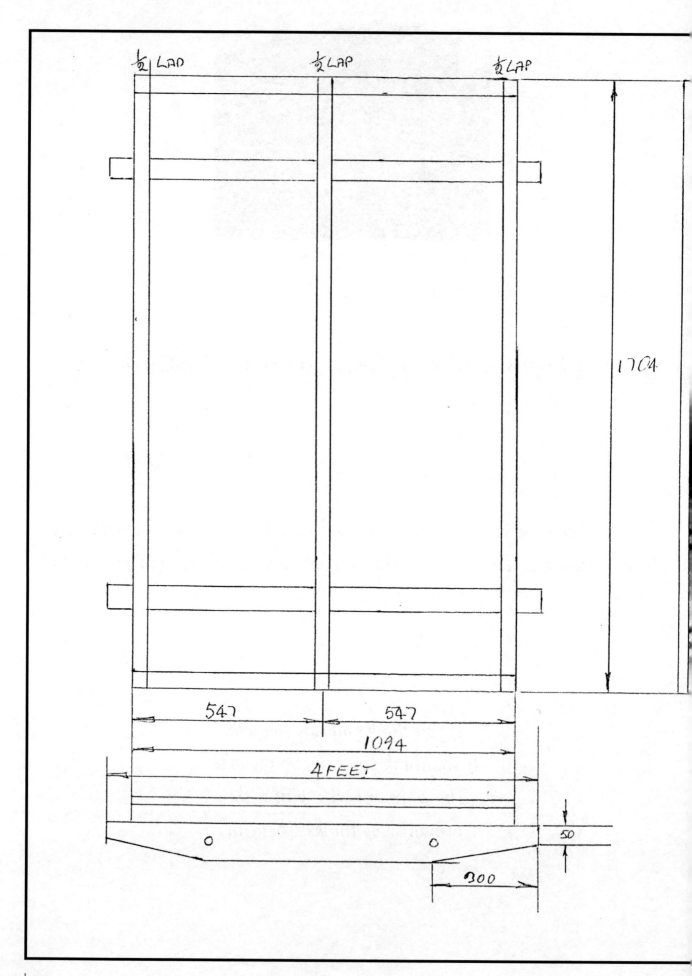

PORTABLE beehouse
4 Foot Floor

4 FEET
CRS

MATERIALS

2 OFF   4IN × 2IN   4FT LONG
2 OFF   45 × 34   1094
3 OFF   45 × 34   1704
1 OFF   12 MM PLY   1704 × 1094

| PORTABLE BEEHOUSE |
| 4 FOOT FLOOR |
| DRAWN B.P. MANN |
| DIMENSIONS IN MM |

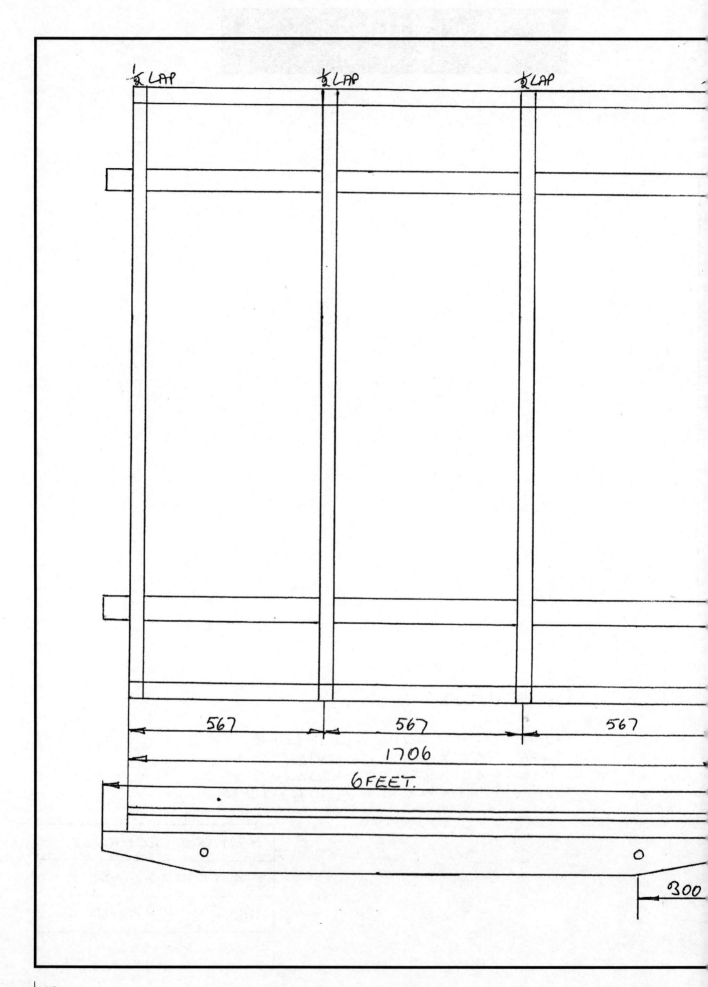

PORTABLE beehouse
6 Foot Floor

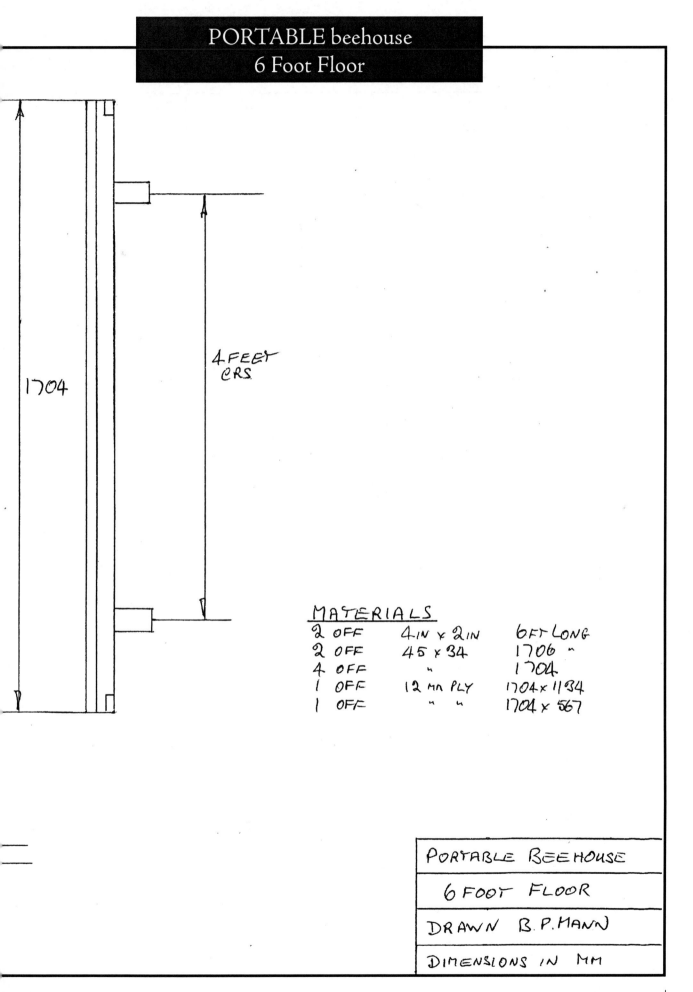

1704

4 FEET
CRS.

MATERIALS
2 OFF   4 IN × 2 IN   6 FT LONG
2 OFF   45 × 34   1706 "
4 OFF   "   1704
1 OFF   12 MM PLY   1704 × 1134
1 OFF   "   "   1704 × 567

PORTABLE BEEHOUSE
6 FOOT FLOOR
DRAWN B. P. MANN
DIMENSIONS IN MM

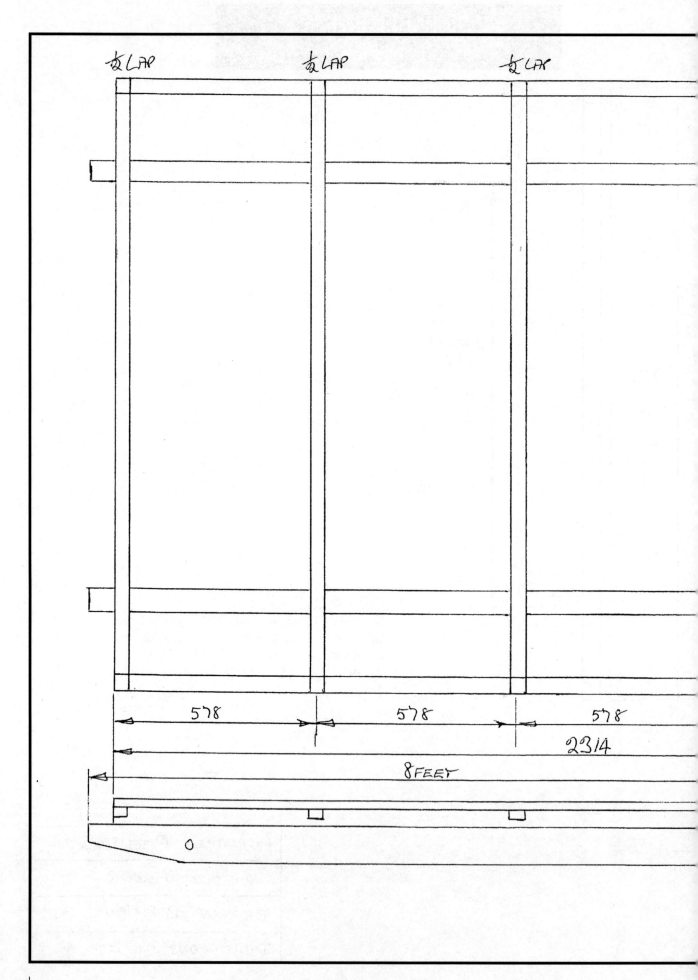

½ LAP   ½ LAP   ½ LAP

578   578   578

2314

8 FEET

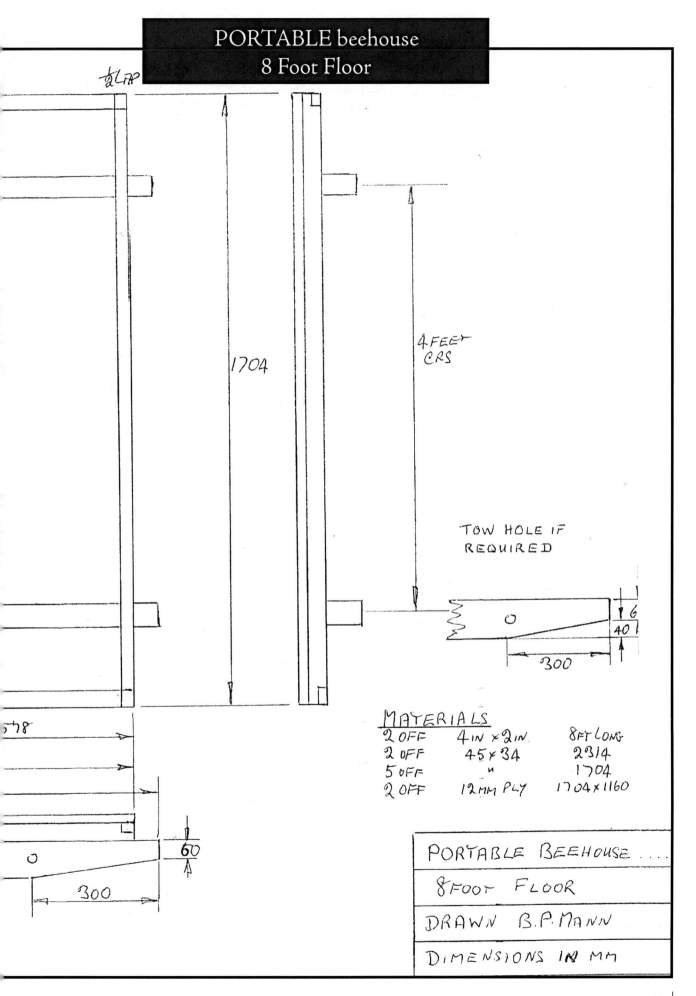

PORTABLE beehouse
8 Foot Floor

½ LAP

1704

4 FEET
CRS

TOW HOLE IF
REQUIRED

6
40
300

578

60
O
300

MATERIALS

2 OFF	4 IN × 2 IN	8 FT LONG
2 OFF	45 × 34	2314
5 OFF	"	1704
2 OFF	12 MM PLY	1704 × 1160

PORTABLE BEEHOUSE ....
8 FOOT FLOOR
DRAWN B.P. MANN
DIMENSIONS IN MM

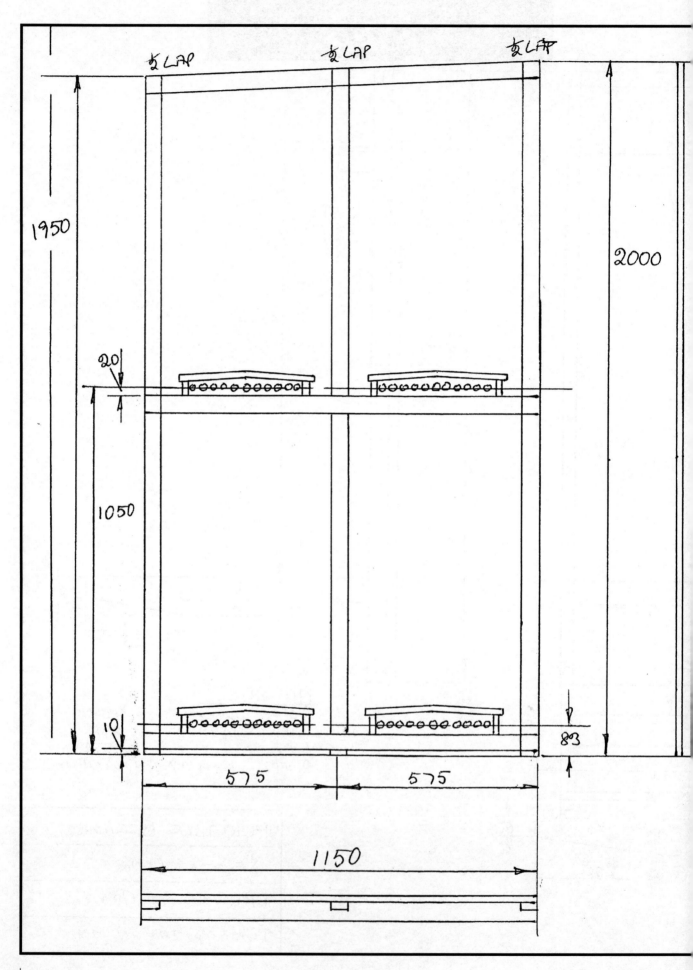

PORTABLE beehouse
4 Foot Sides

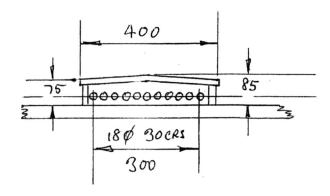

400

75   85

18⌀ 30CRS

300

MATERIALS EACH SIDE

1 OFF   6MM PLY   2000 × 1150
2 OFF   45 × 35   1150
1 OFF   45 × 22   1150
3 OFF   45 × 22   2000 — TRIM AS REQ

ENTRANCES

8 OFF   45 × 16 ×   400
16 OFF   45 × 16   75

PORTABLE BEEHOUSE
4 FT SIDES — 2 REQ — HANDED
DRAWN B.P. MANN
DIMENSIONS IN MM

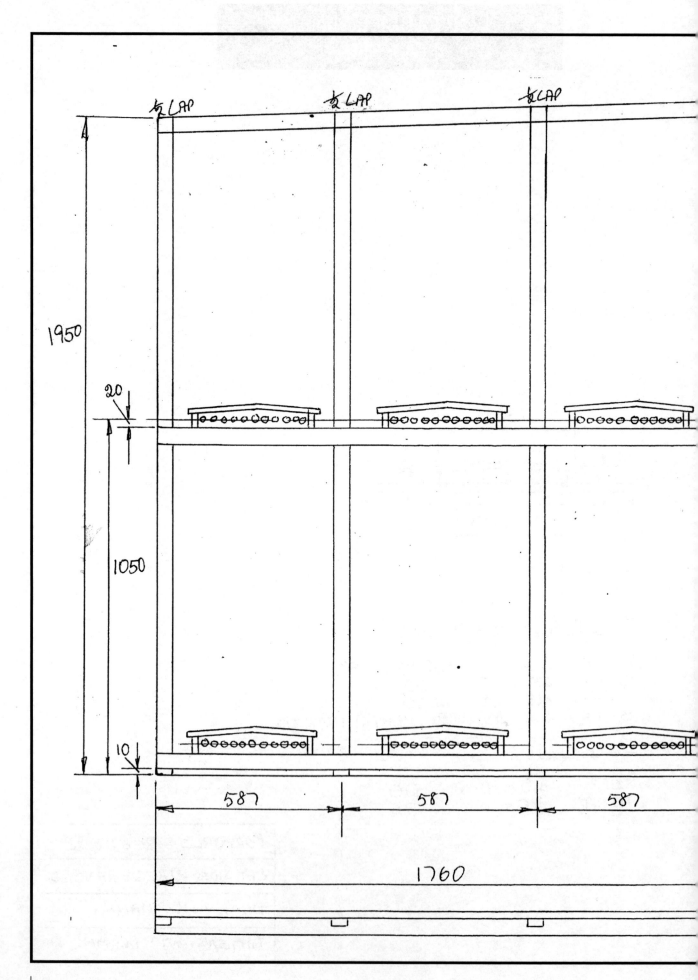

PORTABLE beehouse
8 Foot Sides

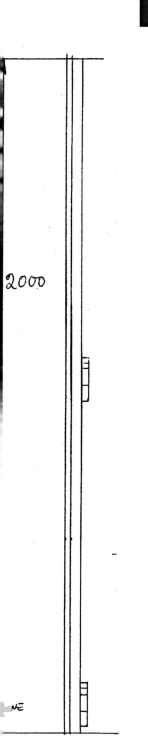

2000

ME

<u>MATERIALS – EACH SIDE</u>

- 1 OFF   6mm. PLY   2000 × 1174
- 1 OFF   6mm PLY   2000 × 587
- 2 OFF   45 × 35   1760
- 4 OFF   45 × 22   2000   TRIM AS REQ
- 1 OFF   45 × 22   1760

<u>ENTRANCES</u>

- 12 OFF   45 × 16   ADD
- 24 OFF   45 × 16   75

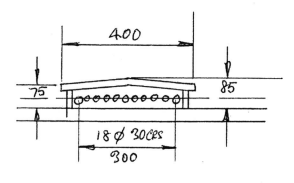

PORTABLE BEEHOUSE	
6FT SIDES 2 REQ – HANDED	
DRAWN B.P. MANN	
DIMENSION IN MM	

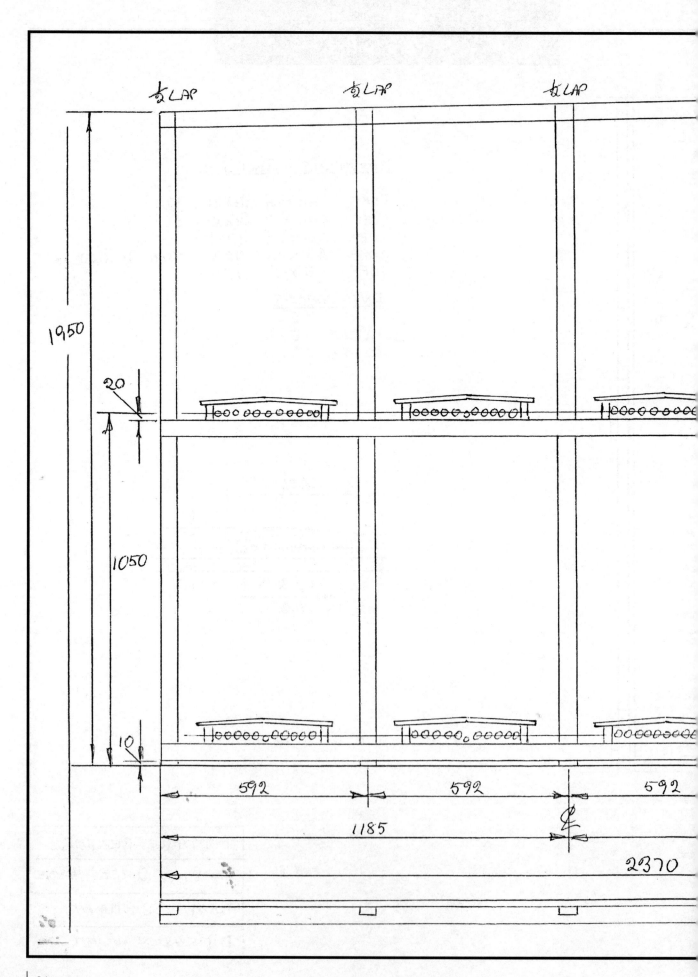

PORTABLE beehouse
8 Foot Sides

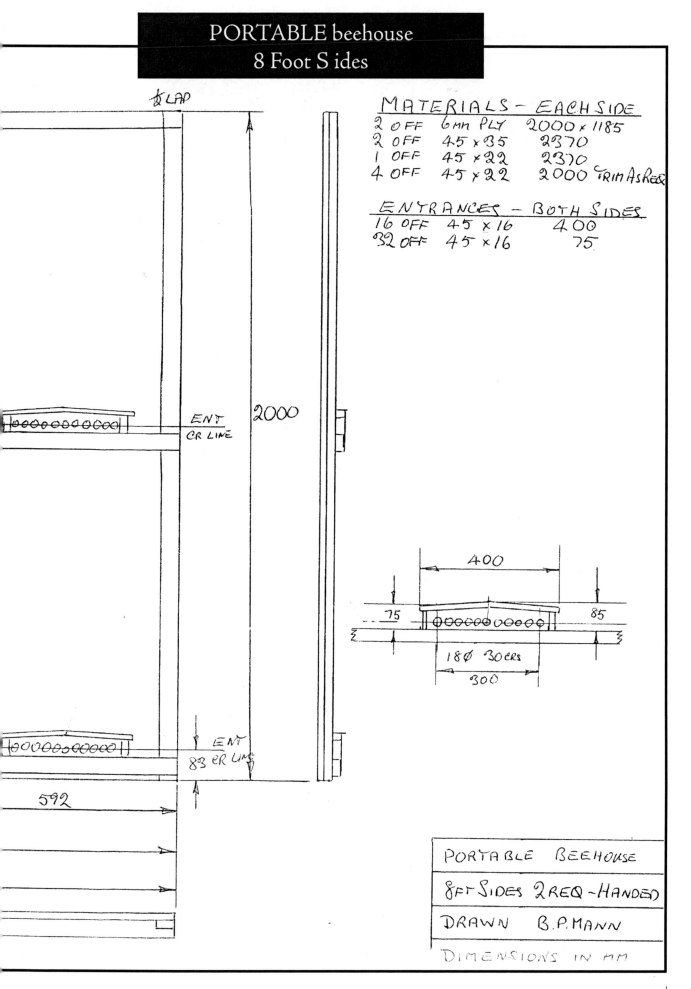

½ LAP

MATERIALS – EACH SIDE
2 OFF 6MM PLY 2000 × 1185
2 OFF 45 × 35 2370
1 OFF 45 × 22 2370
4 OFF 45 × 22 2000 TRIM AS REQ

ENTRANCES – BOTH SIDES
16 OFF 45 × 16 400
32 OFF 45 × 16 75

ENT
CR LINE

2000

ENT
83 CR LINE

592

400

75   85

18∅ 30 CRS

300

PORTABLE BEEHOUSE

8 FT SIDES 2 REQ – HANDED

DRAWN B.P. MANN

DIMENSIONS IN MM

Back joined to floor

Two sides added, the author is on the right standing up. A very good friend, Jozef
Cych [R.I.P.], on the left, helped with these constructions. He was born in Lodz, in
Poland, and spent his early years there during the war.

DOOR END

This part is similar to the sides and best achieved on a flat surface. The door is nominally 2 feet [600mm] wide, this makes
the carrying of boxes possible without catching your knuckle on the side. A hook and eye to hold the door open is well
worth while. Occasionally a gust of wind will whip the door round on you. Likewise a means of closing the door from the
inside is useful in cool weather.

ROOF

If this is assembled as one piece it does get quite heavy. Two of us were able to get the complete roof onto the top of the sided
and ends. Consider how much help you will get when the time comes to put the roof on. It is quite possible to assemble the
roof in two parts and then complete the assembly on top of the beehouse. It is possible to get chipboard with a pre-coating
of roofing felt already applied. Alternatively you can use ply, you have a choice. Cut the full panel into two lengthwise, fix the
edge batten and the side bar of the opening with screws or ring nails. At this stage the two parts can be put onto the top of
the beehouse and the construction completed in this position.

When all the timber work and felting have been finished fit the 5 cross bars to support the clear sheet. Special kits
of fixings are made so that the screws go through the top of the corrugations, a support tube fits underneath the sheet and
special cups hold the top of the screw, a cap closes over the head of the screw, it is then all water tight If you can fit a gutter

and down pipe across the blank end it will take all the water from the roof down to ground level. This keeps the back of the beehouse dry. Screw the edges of the roof to the top edge of the sides and ends. This makes the structure more rigid and prevents the roof being blown off in a gale!!

As I have said the plans have been tested and all dimensions are correct. However you may wish to make an alteration of your own. This is fine but do be aware that changing one dimension or changing the section of a piece of timber may require you to alter other dimensions. Remember my fathers advice to measure things twice or even more times and then cutting it once. I have come to appreciate how good this motto is. Please do not ask how!!!

If you decide to have a beehouse then this will require thought. For a few hives on the floor then normal hives are quite satisfactory. The main disadvantage is the extra cost of the hives and the beehouse. To make maximum use of the space I used hives on the floor each side and again about half way up. The hives on the floor can be inspected by kneeling down and the shelf hives while standing up. Space is a bit limited but I found I soon got used to working in a beehouse. Human beings are very adaptable.

For the upper layer of hives I found that the coffin boxes were very satisfactory, so much so that I used a similar construction for the bottom layer. This is clearly seen in the picture on page 9. Plans are in this book for British Standard, British Commercial and Langstroth. Please note that the Langstroth plan has NOT been tested, if you find a mistake please let me know. If you wish to use the 14 X 12 type of frame or the Modified Dadant, also known as the Langstroth deep then all you need to do is to increase the depth dimensions to match.

It is very tempting to alter dimensions when making brood chambers and supers. Do be careful. The bee space, [1/4 to 3/8 inches or 6 to 10mm] is very important around frames and between boxes and queen excluders. If they are not correct you will have trouble getting frames "IN" or "OUT" of the boxes because of Propolis or "burr" comb. Getting this correct before is much easier than trying to alter it afterwards. Ask any beekeeper.

The side pieces were from 12mm ply and the floor from 6mm ply. These are held together by pieces of 1 X 1 [25 X 25], use rust proof screws then you will then get a very substantial trough in which to place the dividers to produce the require number of brood boxes. The very important dimension is that between the dividers as this sets the bee spaces to the ends of the frames. I recommend that you cut a piece of suitable timber to form a gauge; then all your dimensions will be the same. I have found that timber is good enough to form supports for the frames. If you wish to use metal or plastic for the runners then you will need to match the dimension so that your "top" or "bottom" bee space is correct. Use a made up frame to act as a check as you go along. There is nothing worse than to get the bee spaces incorrect and then the bees either stick the frames to the box or fill a gap with Propolis or comb. You have bee warned.

When making any type of box to contain "frames" then the internal dimension is most important. Never work from an external dimension inwards. This is asking for trouble.

ADVANTAGES.

The beekeeper enters the beehouse and the bees are not aware that the beekeeper is there. You can open the colony without bothering about the flying bees Foragers will return to the entrance as normal and not see a person at all nor will they when they are inside the hive. This is the case even when it is raining. If there is a strong wind then this does not affect the beekeeper inside. Any bees that leave the combs fly quickly to the light above and then escape. In a built up area the neighbours are not aware that there are bees in the beehouse. Mr Ted Crimmins [RIP] of Southport wrote an article in Beekeeping Quarterly Issue No 13 April 1988, he was very close to his neighbours and they used to watch him with binoculars, this annoyed him somewhat. He put a nylon mesh screen around the front of his beehouse, about 4 feet away so that the bees had to fly upwards and so over the surrounding gardens so as not to bother his neighbours. He could then work inside his beehouse without being seen. He was delighted with the result.

The bees are not obvious in a beehouse so that vandalism is unlikely. Theft would be very difficult under normal circumstances.

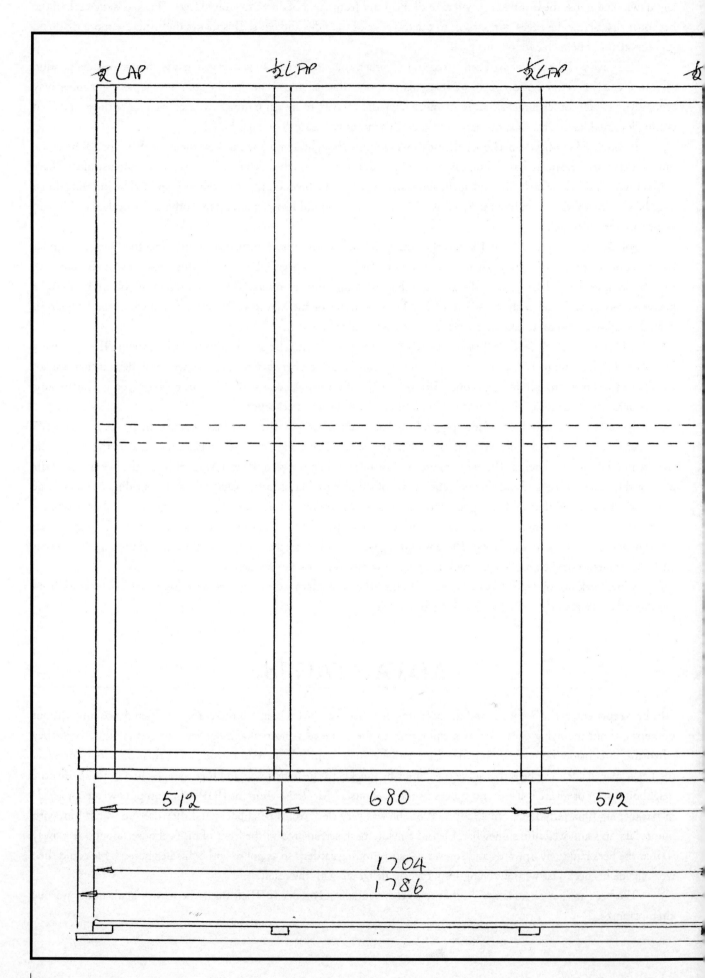

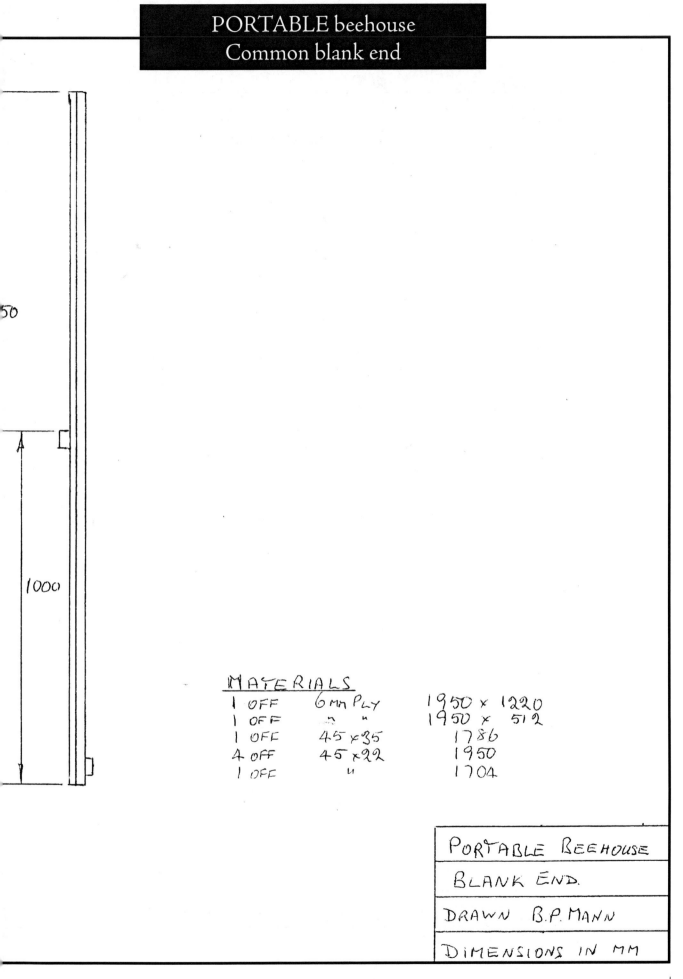

PORTABLE beehouse
Common blank end

50

1000

MATERIALS
1 OFF   6MM PLY   1950 × 1220
1 OFF   "   "   1950 × 512
1 OFF   45×35   1786
4 OFF   45×22   1950
1 OFF   "   1704

PORTABLE BEEHOUSE	
BLANK END.	
DRAWN B.P. MANN	
DIMENSIONS IN MM	

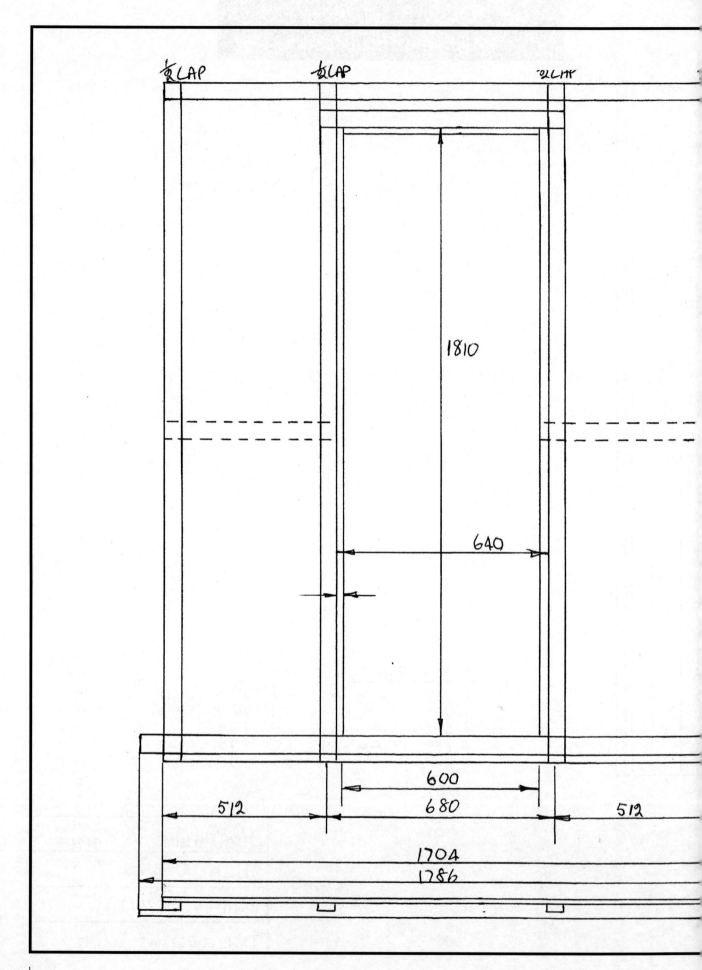

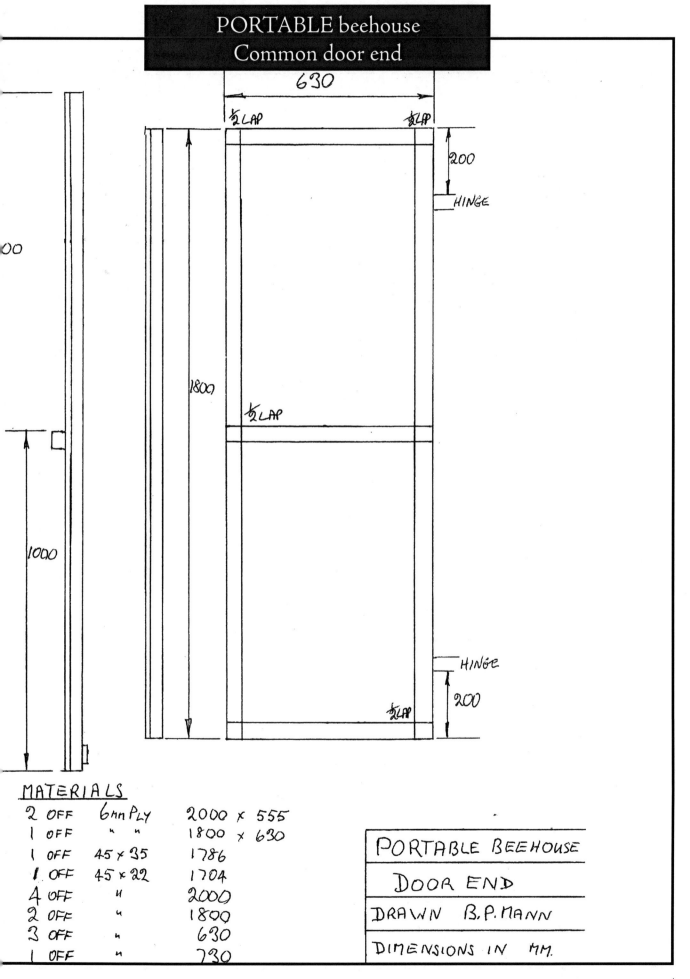

630

½ LAP   ½ LAP

200

HINGE

1800

½ LAP

00

1000

HINGE

200

½ LAP

MATERIALS

2 OFF	6mm PLY	2000 x 555
1 OFF	" "	1800 x 630
1 OFF	45 x 35	1786
1 OFF	45 x 22	1704
4 OFF	"	2000
2 OFF	"	1800
3 OFF	"	630
1 OFF	"	730

PORTABLE BEEHOUSE
DOOR END
DRAWN B.P.MANN
DIMENSIONS IN MM.

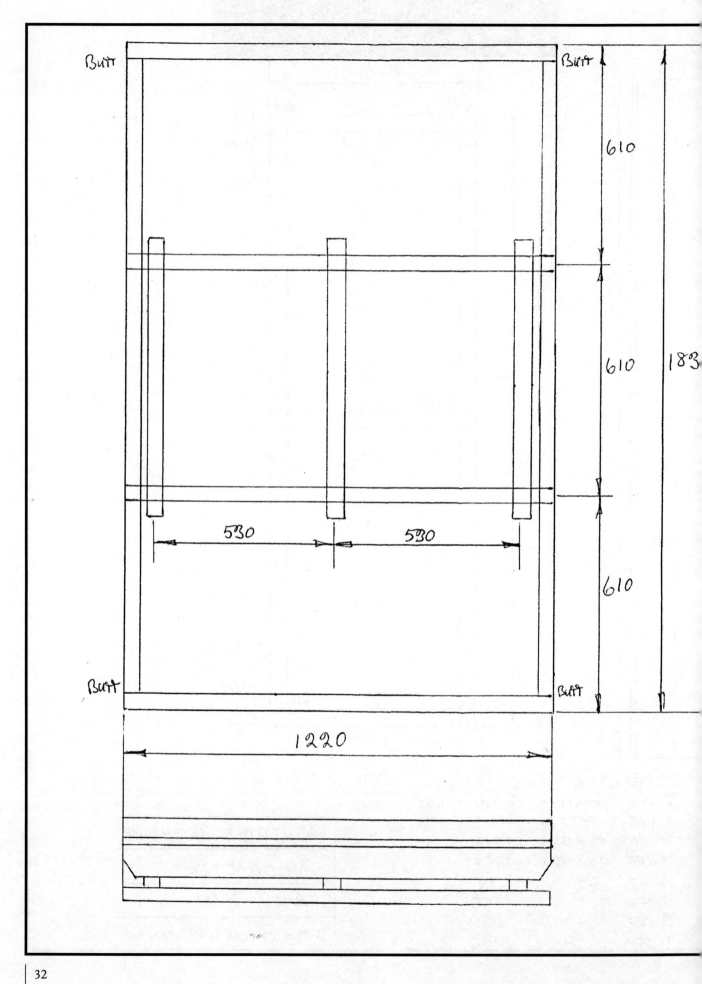

PORTABLE beehouse
4 Roof

MATERIALS

	1 OFF	4FT × 4FT	PREPELTED CHIPBOARD
OR	1 OFF	4FT × 4FT	12mm PLY
	2 OFF	45 × 35	1220
	2 OFF	45 × 35	1760
	2 OFF	95 × 27	1220
	2 OFF	95 × 27	630
	3 OFF	45 × 22	765
	1 OFF	4FT × 2FT 6IN	CORR PLASTIC

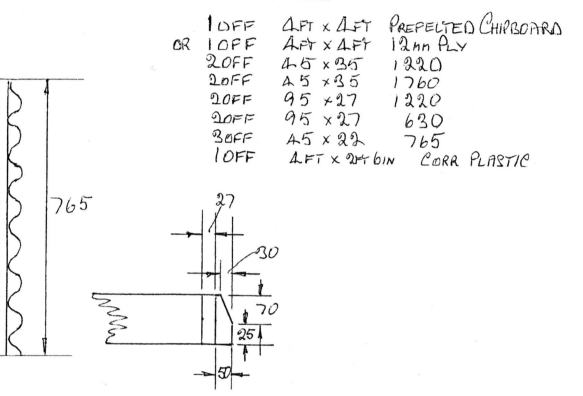

765

27
30
70
25
50

PORTABLE BEEHOUSE
4 FOOT ROOF
DRAWN B. P. MANN
DIMENSIONS IN MM

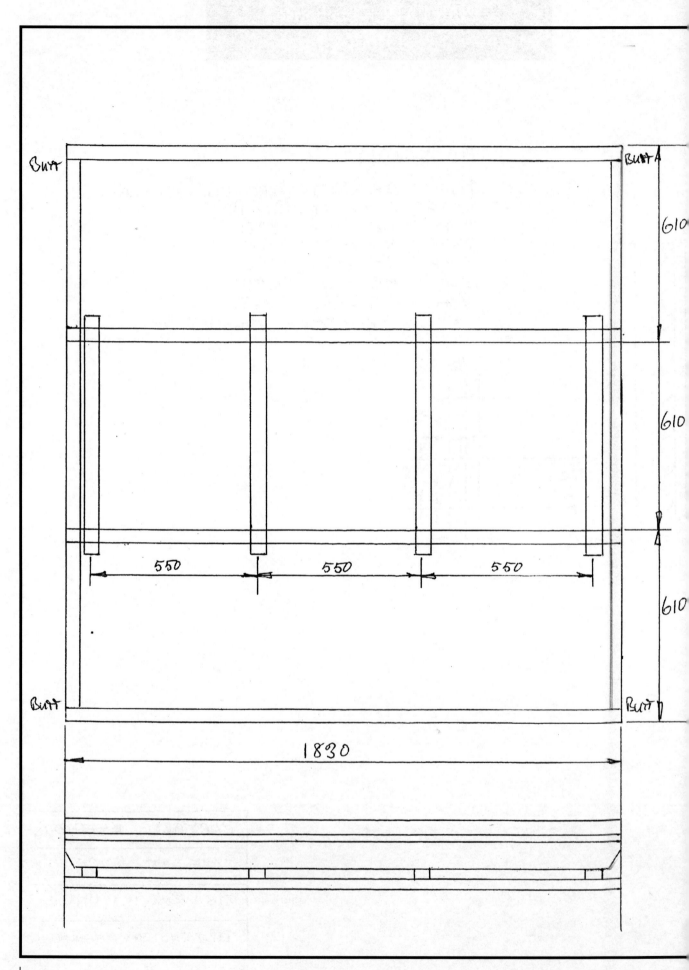

PORTABLE beehouse
6 Roof

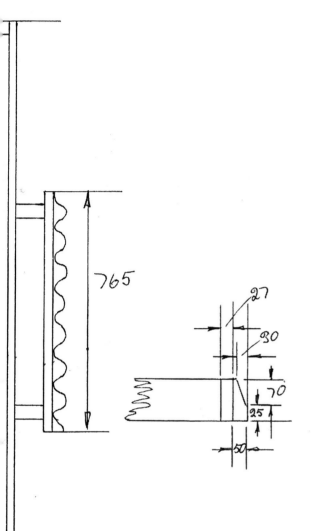

765

27

30

70

25

50

MATERIALS

1 OFF	6 FT × 4 FT	PRE-FELTED CHIPBOARD
OR 1 OFF	6 FT × 4 FT	12 mm PLY
2 OFF	45 × 35	1830
2 OFF	45 × 35	1760
2 OFF	95 × 27	1830
2 OFF	95 × 27	630
4 OFF	45 × 22	765
1 OFF	6 FT × 2 FT 6 IN	CORR PLASTIC

PORTABLE BEEHOUSE
6 FOOT ROOF
DRAWN B. P. MANN
DIMENSIONS IN MM

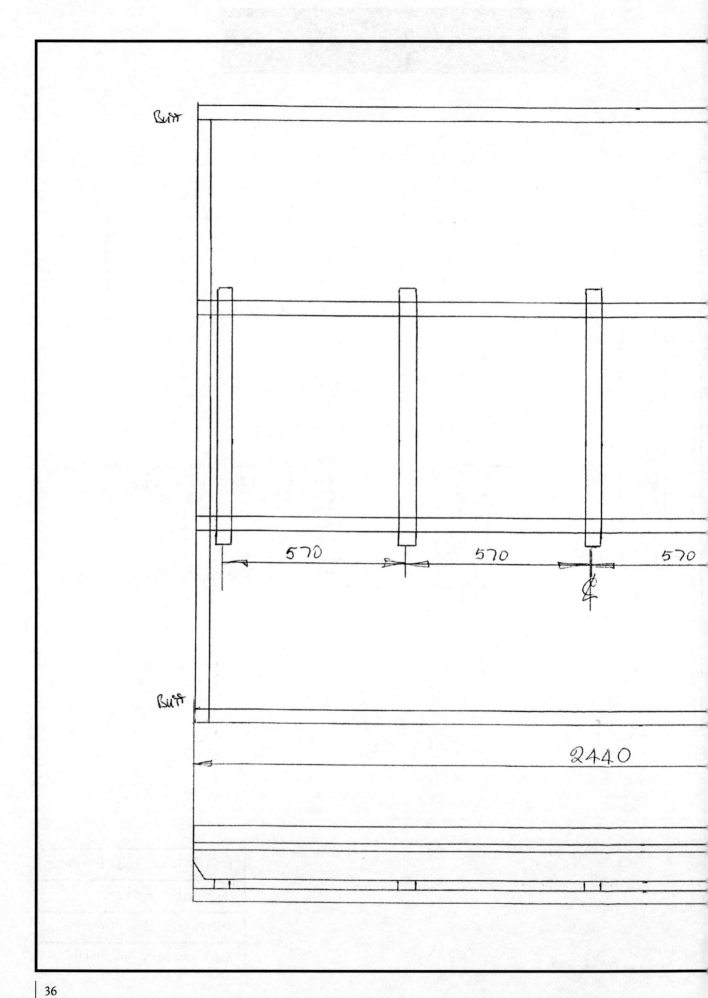

PORTABLE beehouse
8 Roof

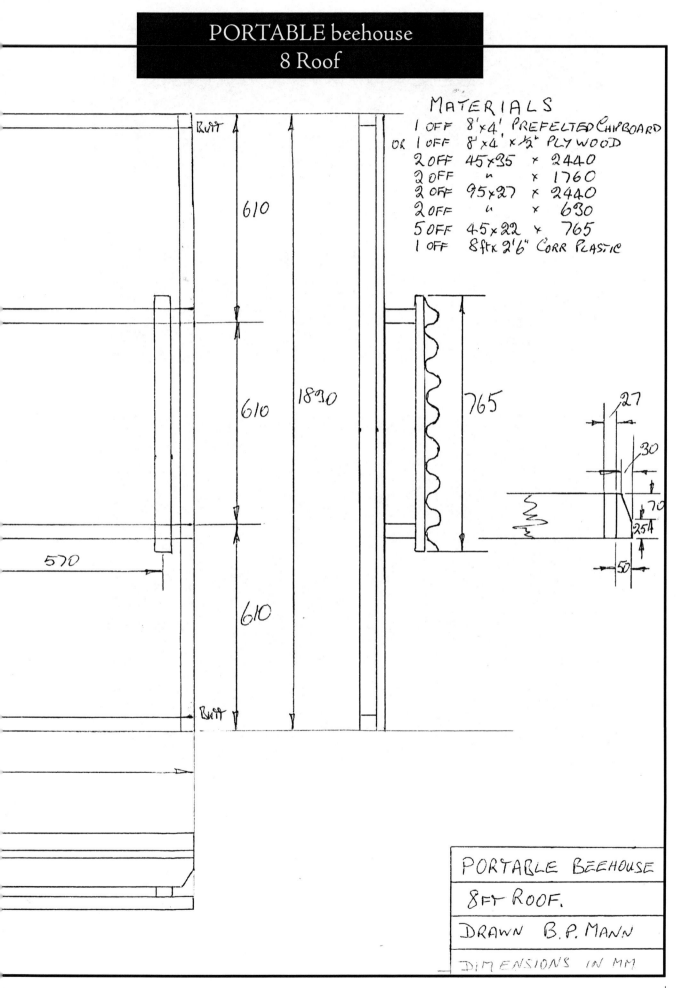

MATERIALS
1 OFF 8'x4' PREFELTED CHIPBOARD
OR 1 OFF 8'x4' x ½" PLYWOOD
2 OFF 45x95 x 2440
2 OFF " x 1760
2 OFF 95x27 x 2440
2 OFF " x 630
5 OFF 45x22 x 765
1 OFF 8ft x 2'6" CORR PLASTIC

BUTT
610
610
1890
765
610
BUTT
570
27
30
70
254
50

PORTABLE BEEHOUSE
8FT ROOF.
DRAWN B.P. MANN
DIMENSIONS IN MM

Floors and dividers to form four brood chambers

Showing a shelf unit inside a beehouse

Showing floor and shelf units fitted into a beehouse

Interior of prototype - show entrances and shelf support

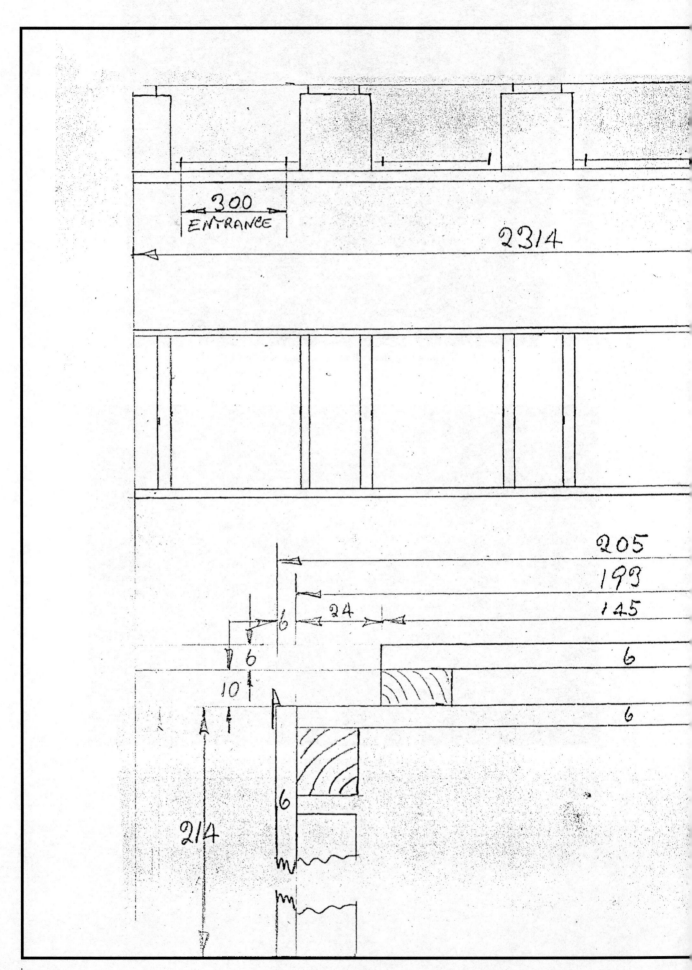

PORTABLE beehouse
British Standard Brood Chamber

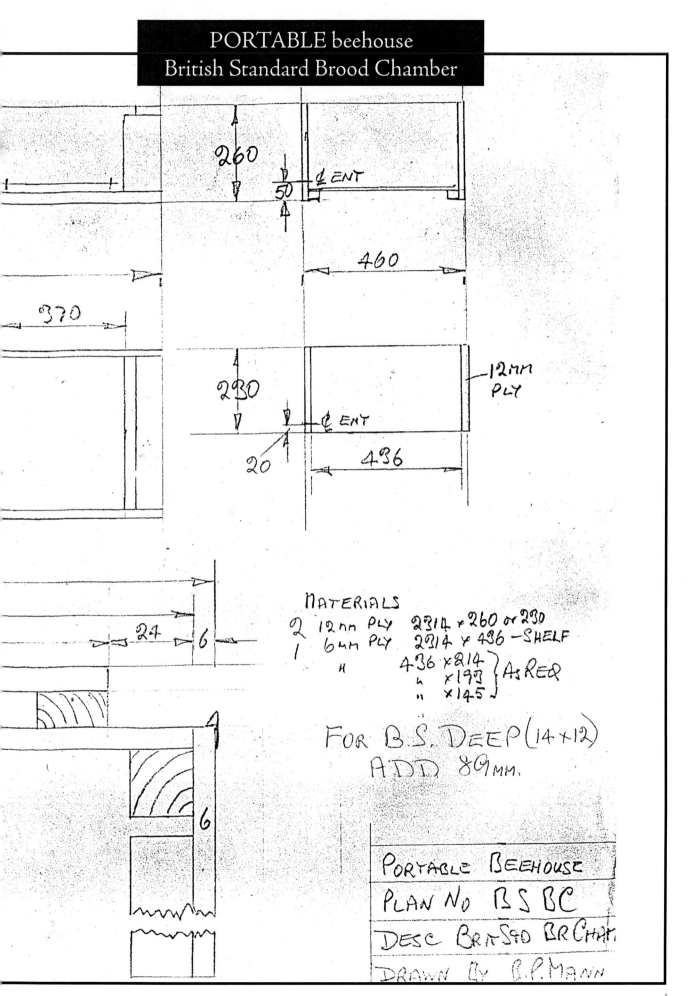

260

50 ⊄ ENT

460

370

230

⊄ ENT

20

496

12MM PLY

24   6

6

6

MATERIALS
2 12MM PLY   2314 × 260 or 230
1 6MM PLY   2314 × 496 —SHELF
   "   436 × 214 ⎫
   "   × 193 ⎬ As REQ
   "   × 145 ⎭

FOR B.S. DEEP (14 × 12)
ADD 89MM.

PORTABLE BEEHOUSE
PLAN No BSBC
DESC BRASSO BR CHAM
DRAWN BY B.P. MANN

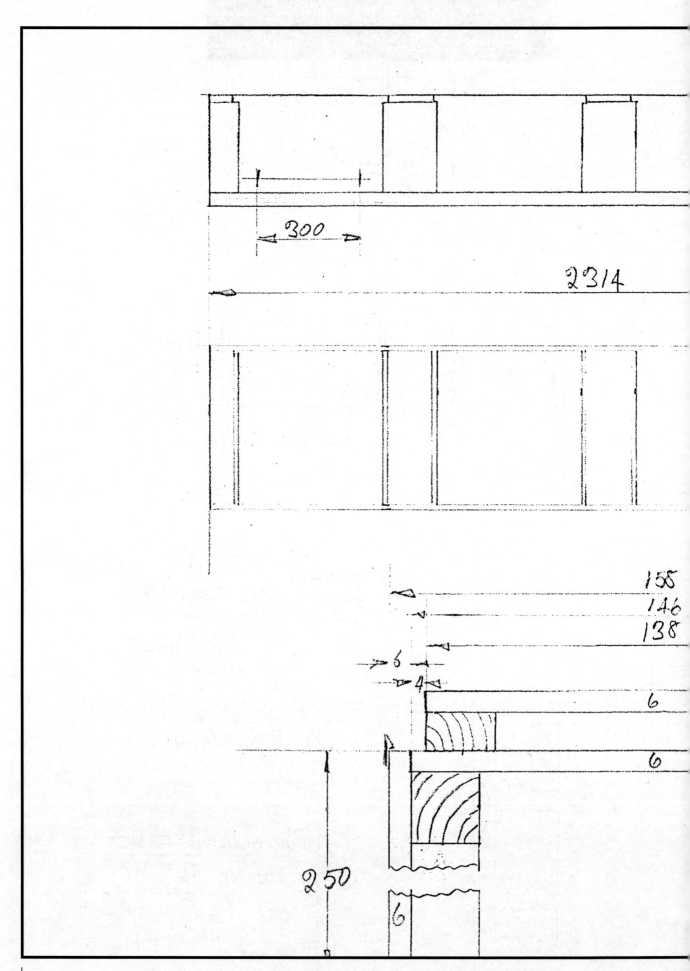

PORTABLE beehouse
British Commercial Brood Chamber

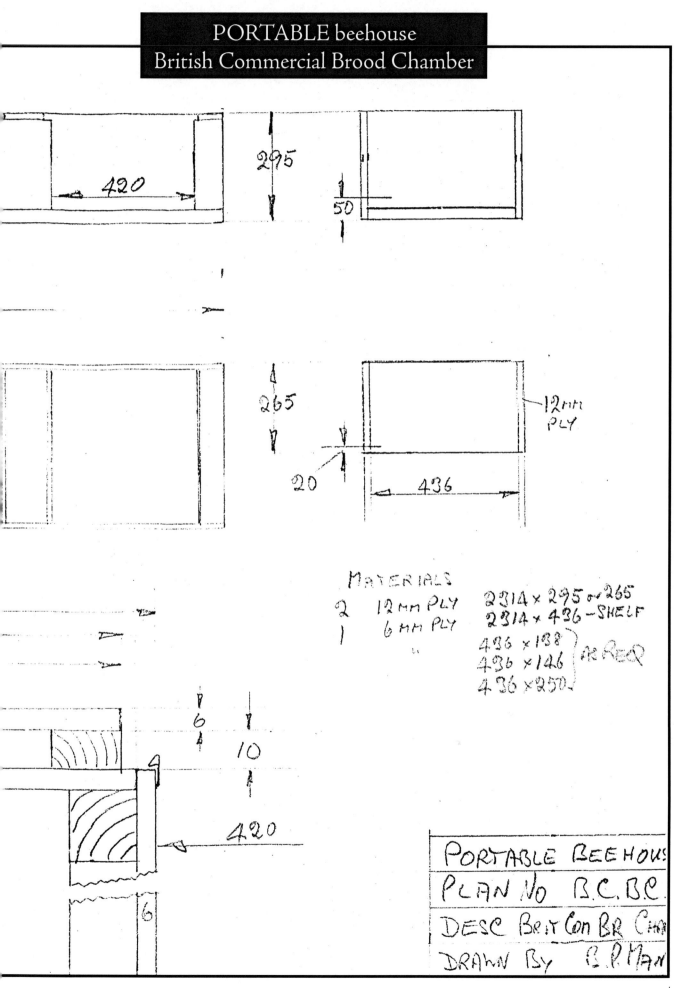

295

420

50

265

20

436

12mm PLY

MATERIALS
2 12mm PLY   2314 × 295 or 265
1 6mm PLY   2314 × 436 - SHELF
             436 × 138 } At REAR
             436 × 146 }
             436 × 250 }

6

10

420

6

PORTABLE BEEHOUS
PLAN No B.C.B.C.
DESC Brit Con Br Cha
DRAWN By C.P.Man

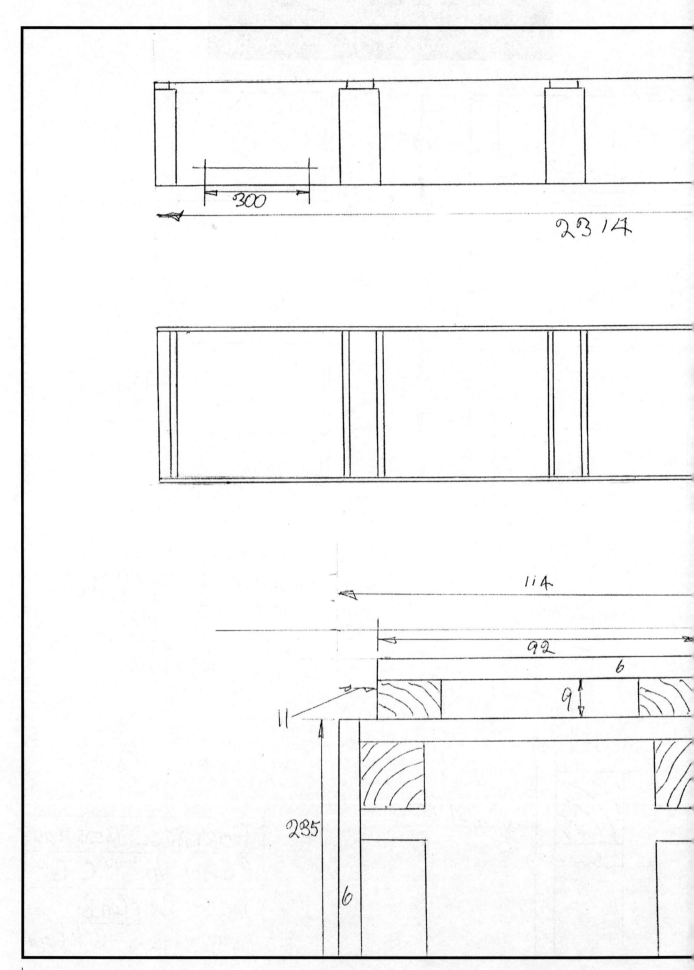

PORTABLE beehouse
Longstroth   Brood Chamber

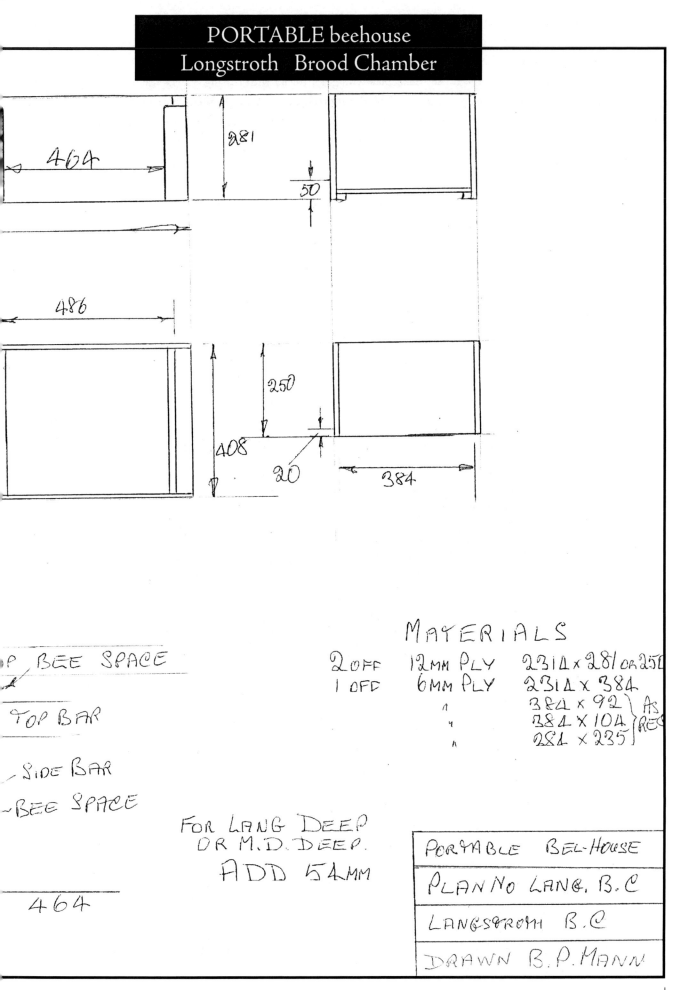

464

281

50

486

250

408

20

384

BEE SPACE

TOP BAR

SIDE BAR

BEE SPACE

FOR LANG DEEP
OR M.D. DEEP.
ADD 54MM

464

MATERIALS

2 OFF   12MM PLY   231Δ × 281 OR 25
1 OFF   6MM PLY   231Δ × 384
                   384 × 92 } AS
                   384 × 104 } RE
                   281 × 235 }

PORTABLE   BEE-HOUSE
PLAN No LANG. B.C
LANGSTROTH B.C
DRAWN B. P. MANN

For the migratory beekeeper the ability to move a number of colonies within a beehouse, could be very advantageous. Care would be needed to have room to manoeuvre vehicles and beehouses at the home and migratory sites. Again theft and vandalism would be more difficult.

QUEEN REARING.   For those beekeepers who get involved with rearing queens then a beehouse becomes really useful because the hives can be opened at any time, almost irrespective of the weather. Once queen cells are started off a strict time-table must be followed. Cells must be separated before the queens emerge and mating units must be made up as soon as the cells are ripe or the virgin queens emerge. All of this can be carried out inside a beehouse.

My own method has been to establish a powerful colony in two brood chambers. If the queen is driven down into the lower box and a queen excluder placed in between. The top box can then be used to provide bees for a swarm box which is an excellent way of getting cells started. After 24 hours the cells can be placed back in the top box and the colony will nurture them until they are used as ripe cells or are separated and the virgins queens allowed to emerge.

Nuclei or mini-nucs can be made up inside from bees out of the colonies within the beehouse. The mating units must then be placed outside while the queens mate.

I did find that queenless colonies would realise there was a queen right colony in a neighbouring hive and walk across and join that colony. External dividers may help to prevent this problem.

No roofs are required in a beehouse but the hives must be bee tight to prevent them using the beehouse roof as an exit and entry point.

Commercial beekeepers are regularly moving numbers of colonies around and this is very strenuous work .Some have built mobile apiaries on a truck or trailer. One is shown in the picture below. I had thought that my beehouses could be used in this way, A flat bed trailer could be used to carry a beehouse from site to site."

DISADVANTAGES OF BEEHOUSES

If you have hives in the multiple colony boxes is not possible to "heft" [lift to check weight] individual colonies so that winter stores must be decided by visual means.

Moving individual colonies into a beehouse is best achieved by placing the normal hive or travelling box outside as near as possible to the eventual entrance and leaving them for a day or two. It is then a simple task to take the box into the beehouse and transfer the combs into the internal hive. Like wise to remove a single colony it is necessary to put them into a hive or travelling box to reverse the process.

I do not think that honey crops are any better or worse in a beehouse, the bees are not able to see the beekeeper taking their honey so it may help to reduce robbing.   Wintering is not affected by the bees being inside. If the beekeeper thinks it is worthwhile then insulation can be draped over the hives. Yes I have done this but only during the spring build up.

With some bees working on one colony may alert others, any vibration will travel. There is very little room to store any loose equipment, a separate store shed is really essential.

PORTABILITY.

All the beehouses I have made and sold were sectional so that transport and erection were not a problem. A second pair of hands makes the task much easier.

To make the beehouses transportable they need to be on "skids" so that they can be moved over the ground easily. A winch or a vehicle can then be used to pull them along. They can be loaded onto a trailer or a flat bed truck. All the sections of the beehouse need to be securely fastened together. I have found that through bolts are the best as the parts are clamped together. Set Screws with a square or hexagonal head are much better than screws driven by a slot or "Phillips" head. The last thing you want is things to start coming apart while you are transporting a beehouse full of colonies.

Internally the "hives" should be clamped together, ratchet straps are very good.

A MODIFIED SHED INTO A BEEHOUSE.

Circumstances recently made it desirable that I have another beehouse. My new site is not really suitable for the use of normal hives. I have always realised that it would be possible to adapt a garden shed to fulfil my design requirements. My first thoughts were an apex roof and then to put a clear roof over the middle. In the end I decided to see if a shed manufacturer would modify one of their basic buildings to my requirements. I was very impressed when I asked S & N Timber of Wallisdown Road in Bournemouth if this was possible. A very quick "Yes" gave them an order. You will see from the photographs what has been achieved. As I already have normal hives and I do not intend to keep a large number of colonies I am using normal hives on the floor only.

I hope I have convinced you of the advantages of having your colonies within a beehouse. I suggest that you go into any shed or building without a roof to get a feel of the amount of light available when it can come in through the top, I still find it amazing. With more and more beekeepers keeping bees in an urban area I can see that beehouses could solve many of their problems. If I have helped to solve the two main problems of keeping bees inside buildings then these notes will be well worth while.

I hope all beekeepers, present and future will find as much pleasure as I have had from their hobby or part time occupation. I tell newcomers that beekeeping is a disease and if you become infected then you will be a beekeeper for the rest of your life. I admire all the commercial beekeepers for the work they do, especially during the summer months. To cope with 2 to 4 hundred colonies during this time is a great achievement. Happy beekeeping to all.

Shed construction February 2010

Nearing completion - author at work!

Roof detail

The Langstroth Hives are standing on a mesh floor with 3 inch (5mm) gap under

Completed entrances

Entrance Detail - A peice of ply will slide across to reduce or close the entrance

Entrance prior to porch

"If only those of us were "here" that were intended to be "here"
then half of us would be missing."

"Let s(he) who thinks themselves indispensable place a thumb in a
mug of water. Remove the thumb and see the hole is leaves."

"We were not experts therefore we did not know what could be done"
David Hutchings [R.I.P.] A canal rescue person.

Lightning Source UK Ltd.
Milton Keynes UK
UKOW012238111012

200406UK00002B/2/P